TWELVE

CLOCKS

Camino del Sol

A Latina and Latino Literary Series

TWELVE

CLOCKS

JULIE SOPHIA PAEGLE

THE UNIVERSITY OF
ARIZONA PRESS

TUCSON

The University of Arizona Press
www.uapress.arizona.edu

Printed in the United States of America
20   19   18   17   16   15   6   5   4   3   2   1

ISBN-13: 978-0-8165-3136-3 (paper)

Cover designed by Leigh McDonald
Cover photo by Leigh McDonald

Publication of this book is made possible in part by the proceeds of a permanent endowment created
with the assistance of a Challenge Grant from the National Endowment for the Humanities, a federal agency.

Library of Congress Cataloging-in-Publication Data
Paegle, Julie Sophia, 1971– author.
  Twelve clocks / Julie Sophia Paegle.
    pages cm — (Camino del sol)
  ISBN 978-0-8165-3136-3 (pbk. : alk. paper)
  1. Time—Poetry. I. Title. II. Series: Camino del sol.
  PS3616.A3363T97 2015
  811'.6—dc23
                    2014024128

♾ This paper meets the requirements of ANSI/NISO Z39.48-1992 (Permanence of Paper).

for Steve, Connor, and Quinn

Y no comprendo cómo el tiempo pasa,
Yo, que soy tiempo y sangre y agonía.

—Jorge Luis Borges, "Adrogué"

Are space and time like a canvas onto which an artist paints; they exist whether or not the artist paints on them? Or are they akin to parenthood; there is no parenthood until there are parents and children?

—John D. Norton

CLOCKWORKS

TWELVE

CLOCKS

Invocation: Calling Calliope with a Midwife's Doppler

spell our lip synch   this shift   help us hear it   apart
help us spell out   from some rivers' blood
the twice faster pulse   small opposite heart

eavesdropping   on the body's call
and response   to find pattern   inside
pattern   silence guiding silence   an arrival

ongoing in true dark   when the body opens
breath is imminent   sky everywhere outside
usher usher life awash in   diligent listening crimsons

Obelisk

The tower takes the sun to make a shadow.   The shadow takes its tower to climb the sky.
The sky takes the tower to thicken zephyr.   Zenith rides its quartz back down to shadow.
The shadow takes a diviner to see the sun.   The diviner takes the shadow to divide day:

before   meridian   after.

Before takes after to scatter hours: an even ten,   two slighter twilights.

Division makes duration, takes its worth.

The tower takes itself to make a city.   The city takes the tower to bide its time.
The city's women take their time to bide its births.

The earth takes the sun to make a shadow.   The shadow takes its earth, devises night.
The night takes the earth and half its towers.   The earth divides the towers: twilight slides.
Twilight takes time from its diviners.   Dawn takes the earth from its half-light.
Between half-lights day casts surface dearth.

The prophet takes up her cause with the diviners.   Night takes the earth.

Commonplace for prophets: *You are in the wrong place or the wrong time.*

I.

NIGHT TAKES THE EARTH

With its neon blazing around the clock, today's Las Vegas—originally settled by Mormon missionaries in 1855—looks like an exotic jewel dropped in the Mojave desert.

—*One Planet*

I know I should see the city like this: excess,
electricity, and excrement daubing the Mojave—
should berate so much waste smeared across

the landscape, should lament a noon laced with unsavory
awakenings—*who sent her?*—and aftertastes; should mind
the collective hangover souring the air. Instead, as we

(too early for check-in) stroll the Strip, lights ascend
or cascade the sky; corners pour diamonds; die-cast
stardust gilds a gila monster on her own island,

watering palms that in this moment suggest
less the casino with the "topless" theme
(its billboard features a woman undressed

except for lipstick and some lettering,
Shhh . . . what happened at the Palms never happened)
than the psychic palm reading

outside my old high school, primly upwind
from prediction-addicted smokers, back in Utah.
She once took a ten from my hand,

ignored its palm lines, and hissed, *What I saw*
is your mother telling you not to smoke pot.
Before this, each of my palms was a jigsaw

puzzle of past and future jumbled together but writ
manageably small, a plot sketched in lines of life/love:
how many babies, jobs, though admittedly not

predicting natural disasters (now hurricanes churn above
Florida and Jamaica; an earthquake shook the family
ranch in Argentina yesterday. Even here, silts wreak hav-

oc on the Luxor's foundation. Blame the stratigraphy
for obelisk's tilt against the sky—when the light's on
the pyramid it's more visible—a surveyor's catastrophe).

Before the seer took my hand, not one
of these stories had begun; though it could be
that their origins wrinkled on the palm—our son

faintly figured among dim possibility
in a whorl unfurling on a fingertip,
now eight months old, dragged into this fury

of fast flashing madness: the New Strip.
When I was a girl, there was not this New/Old
split, just the street neatly halving our yearly trip

between Salt Lake and LA, between the cold
dim disk of winter's sun and the disco ball
awaiting us in California, dripping its gold

over mazy tinsel Christmas—that scene in Annie Hall
about how Hollywood does holidays gives a fair
picture of the surrealism of it all—

but what can do justice to this middle-of-nowhere
excess? In the seventies, what I wanted was the doll
my grandfather would buy for me and each sister

from that store in Circus Circus, its ten-foot walls
lined from floor to ceiling with the plastic cartons
in which hoop skirts, feathered hats, and lace shawls

were crushed. The dolls evoked salons
lush with swoons—ruffled bustles, lavish low cuts,
eyes huge in ochres and viridians;

earrings and chokers plush jets of black velvet
dotted with sequins; and under layers of satin
slip and dress, high boots laced over fishnet.

The dolls' feathered splendor indisputably took part in
the glamour trailed by the Stardust sign—a breathless
windblown twinkling, part Dulcinea, part Carmen,

probably part Esmeralda, I confess,
but before Disney got hold of her—and part of why
I'm dragging my baby through this overstimulating mess

of traffic and cigarettes and the oversized confetti
of triple X leaflets for Francesca and Ivana Tramp
has something to do with a trick of lost time, memory,

or premonition—my grandfather saw a ramp
in the days before he died, descending to his bed
from the ceiling, so he refused, alongside the pomp

of funeral and wedding, to lie down. He was afraid
of the memories that swirled in to face
him when he closed his eyes, of all those who went instead

of him to death in the war, in each trench, each place
obliterated, like his home, the fields where, still
a boy, he hid when they killed his family. *Las Vegas,*

he was fond of reminding us, means *The Fertile
Valleys. This desert is the memory of a dream
of water.* He'd take his pills, pull the slots, fill

keno cards with our birthdays, and redeem
another year of Stardust stays. He died in the ninth
month of my pregnancy. Now we watch water stream

up to star in its own show, describing stair or labyrinth,
unraveling the mazes it resolves in the air,
waterlight finespun through several lengths,

braiding, unbraiding, following itself where-
ever it arcs, leaps, or falls. Connor loves the show,
reaches for the water, cries when it's over. We share

his wonder. You read from a sign: *Laminar flow
occurs in water from which all turbulence has been removed.
What remains is its ionic force.* It's impossible, I know:

the stuff of oasis pure, compressed; what is loved
in a void but without loss; pleasure with the promise
of no memory, no mess; desire halved

from its price, then removed and kept, its surface
glassy, quite intact, beyond the realm of turbulence—
What happened at the Palms never happened. We pass

the afternoon watching water dance,
far from the eyes of two huge moving storms,
far from the center of an earthquake in the province

where my mother grew up—Catamarca deforms
with practiced ease, after years of floods and droughts
(impossible to imagine those waters tamed to perform).

Now dusk is falling in water's shoots and between zoot-
suited teens, their pachuco-y, vintage, ubiquitous roamings.
We struggle up the Strip, the baby plucking at the lights—

too late to attend opening night of the clock auction
that drew us all here; too late to bid on much less
win the replica of that hourglass fit for a queen,

too late to seek the price of repair on the price-
less, heirloom, intact-so-far clock by the Argentine
clockmaker (our sons will break it into pieces

over the years); too late to show Connor the marine
life that floats eerily beneath the Mandalay Bay,
sharks circling each other in their green

mottled light. Can they sense the way
the weight above them is not all sea and sky,
a kinesthetic premonition of the play

of space pressing down, the specific gravity
above warped by concrete, marble, steel—
the way our future's unseen shaky masonry

sometimes emerges, sudden, ominous, and real,
to dispel the oblivions of the present
like so much fantasy, flimsy before oracle,

omens unfolding forward from each lived instant
to balance memory? Oracles, like warnings,
might be less hidden than ignored, their content

tuned out like the rock, rap, pop lyrics blaring
down on the Strip from speakers concealed but loud,
discrete zones of sound more violent in their jostling

than the human bodies that constitute the crowd.
I try to tune in as we walk (*like a pinch on the neck
from Mister Spock*), but the lyrics attack, then blur and fade,

unsettling as the twin serpents that struck
down Laocoön (*chosen by lot a priest of Neptune*) only to recede
(*gliding to the citadel of cruel Pallas, they hide*). Worse luck

for the prophet and the Trojans who misread
his death, rushed precipitous to meet their wish: ten years
of war become victory. But then, who hasn't hid-

den from a cipher? Cassandra chanted to deaf ears;
our neighbor lied to her son about what it meant
when he met himself descending the stairs.

*I told him he'd live a long, prosperous life—but you can't
reverse your child's fate. He was dead by winter.
I suppose if he'd met himself on the ascent,*

she'd have spoken true. Our son, asleep, begins to stir,
as we punch through an anachronistic trumpet halloo
blaring across yards of red carpet—Excalibur.

A voice shouts, *Aw, I'm in the white man's casino!*
We were heading for the Old Strip, clocks, and dolls,
but nostalgia has been slain by the crossbow

behind the check-in desk. Exhaustion falls
over everything, gilding dragons, slot machines,
medieval trees, 21 tables, suits of armor on the walls,

moving walkways, with the same unearthly shine
as the elevator mirrors. The doors close on a wrist—
quick, insistent—to pinch café con leche skin. They open

on a chime. A girl teeters in. *Is this tower two? I lost
my directions at the auction—can you believe
I don't have the time? My watch is slow, and just*

now—mier-coles, jueves y viernes, she expansively waves
her wrist at us, *it's stopped, no?* A burly stopwatch:
its giant backlit face blazes parallel lines—four or five

—on the air even after she snatches
it back. *My name's Sandra—call me Clare.
You know, Clare de Lune?* And now it reaches

us—the whiff of fresh sweat mixed with L'Air
du Temps, the glitter marring olive skin
mismatched with ice-blonde hair, her

belly's press against the microdress loose on
a shiver-thin frame elsewhere. The too long second
it takes me to construe her situation

hits a resonant frequency with another recent second
when I took the baby to see close up the men clearing
brush roadside (big rigs!) before their pained

foreman shooed me away, *Ma'am, don't rouse the con-
victs.* A bemused Clare de Lune summons pluck,
explains to elevator air, *No one can date the moon.*

*Ma arrière-arrière-grand-mère, Clare, gave me bad luck
but good blood; I auctioned all her things from the island—
firefly cages, sundials, a blue spittoon, divining stick,*

À la recherche du temps perdu . . . She holds her hands.
Her eyes are huge, painted; her heels perforate
carpet. *Vive la Martinique!* A bird rises, expands

behind her chest; can she be thirteen? *I'm late.*
The baby reaches for her. Cooing, she squints
at a scribbled slip before her, shaking in the light,

repeats to herself, *2012.* The numbers glint
and climb. *They didn't exactly ask for me by name—
does it seem like my first time?* It isn't a lament.

Her dress is iridescent crystal with an emerald hem;
her choker a jet of velvet, brilliant indigo.
How do we answer? Eyes behind her palm,

she singsongs to the baby, *I'll take that as a no.*
We rise, ringed with mirrors, with our own
reflections armored, away from the flow

of traffic on the street, the shark's cyan
subterranean circling, the whirling roulette.
Nearby, palm fronds spell the night's fortune

to the sky. It goes like this: a girl is met
by herself in a mirror. She flows upward. She is calm.
Her surface is intact, as befitting the knight

she will become. *O my land, o Ilium*
The doors open. She gives our son a kiss,
for luck. She turns and gallops into flame.

Hourglass

flame-blown surface, hollow as shadow, flows over its amorphous, noncrystalline skin:

sand: deep-time throne in whose flow the mountains' queen at last takes her repose;
glass: windless sea of sand taking the shape of bulb blown down on itself to windlass

pipette: ladder in sand-river, door in the hour: then back to symmetrical expanse: double-funnel:
bell ringing bell: response then call: every outside within one's once and future self:

an obelisk is a sandstone shadow cast off that wall-less room, time;
the hourglass carries its own lasting axis: unfurls ionic tides from its own minute moons: when

night falls or freezes, the sand falls still; all it wants is one to espy the moment when its fall may still:

when the hour is up, unfurled from minute bits of land—

then the spy can simply turn time over—

ringing old riverbeds like a bell—

as glass remembers sand—

and reverse the spell:

        as can be seen in the commonplace for spies: *The Queen is dead, long live the Queen.*

II.

GLASS REMEMBERS SAND

Watchmakers adopted the quartz-crystal resonator from radio transmitters, many of which were incidentally used in espionage for high resolution eavesdropping. When driven by a voltage at its harmonic frequency, the quartz crystal oscillates resonantly, ringing like a bell.

—"A Chronicle of Timekeeping," William J. H. Andrews

Hourglasses were placed on the pulpit and woe betide he who ran over the full two hours. Certain of the clergy did overdo it and during the reign of Queen Victoria an eighteen minute hourglass appeared in her church.

—*Puritan Pleasures*, Heart Humphries and Burl Mercer

The City of Quartz has two loves: watches and spies.

Time itself, passing down the pulpit, assumes the body of

Night: one love roams Belgrano while at home, the other love mirror milongas.

any body moving: a tongue rolling in piety, four ballrooms in quadrille, or

One love is commonly double.

one scullery bound silk stocking. As

Both observe the city, through glass or not.

glass takes in its stain, each thing takes in its time, perhaps

The love shadow is carried away with expansive gestures.

forgetting where one came from, as perhaps

One pockets gestures.

glass forgets sand.

One is piezoelectric.

Each fine grain

falling away from

One is voyeuristic.

others, having passed

One is often on display.

through the hourglass's mouth, its part a fit perfected

Espionage suggests the watch is an unreliable narrator.

for losing sand, for falling time, for smoothing

The watch reliably loses two minutes each day.

roar of what was once ocean, or eggshell, or shore, for keeping

Such jagged dragging intervals are uncommon in quartz.

each sermon moving. A slow sermon offends the Queen.

A slow watch throws off a spy's calculations.

An offended queen may, at any time, begin to make corrections.

A savvy spy may, at any time, begin to make corrections.

The

hour-

glass is turned twice each Sunday

but never with the Queen in attendance,

since her arrival (bells, ostensible) suggests

her own service (prayer in profile): for

these 18 minutes subjects will watch.

Though she might prefer to worship in private,

during the other 1422 minutes, spies will be watch-

ing. Spies come from everywhere, and pray-

ing privately cannot count for this

allegiance of appearances. At times,

on the other side, beyond the curtain, a

spy—forgetting himself as rain in

rain—is moved

to applaud

and/or

amen.

Can one begin watching at 11:10?
They begin watching for her profile

No. That's waiting, not watching.
early, when there are only rumors

It sounds like he's waiting.
that sound like her approach.

Since he's faster.
She's gaining

You wait in
on each

rumor,
your face.

ravishingly
And God's face?

dressed, soon to overpass
There are rumors—

them into the service. They turn the glass
only rumors—but espionage suggests

as soon as she enters; once she's seated, her train
once near midnight, once near noon

arranged, she gives a sign. Then the bells begin—
—you know when—bits of profile flash—

His profile looks like 11:11?

Her profile is incomparable.

Then what's all this about 11:11?

We all know that espionage suggests

there are creatures who cast three-dimensional shadows:

these shadows look very much like you, but only if you could see

—everywhere at once, ringing and ringing

yourself, iridescent, from all directions

—and hear in that ringing the silver river—

passing through the door in the hour

III.

DOOR IN THE HOUR

The queen of Spain called yesterday to express her condolences to President Kirchner, lamenting, *So many young people.*

Thursday's nightclub inferno, at the popular República Cromañón nightclub, killed at least 175 people and injured 619 others. The fire was probably caused by a child between five and ten years old, who had been left in a nursery improvised in the ladies' restroom.

—translation of local Buenos Aires paper dated January 1, 2005

Doorman. I nod—Americana, but
appreciative—weave out into Buenos Aires, the city's
furniture district. Behind, I leave the bite

of my first son's year-old wail. *This is how he
will learn,* I tell myself, *to play with other children.*
I've left him for the first time with a nanny

and nurse, Clara, while she tends three of her seven
children and my grandmother. Just for the hour,
I tell myself, hurrying; *just to read, uninterrupted, even*

*forty-five minutes. Is this time short or long or never enough when the mere fifteen minutes of transition
labor was a bucking frenzy of eternity cut down, rent out in blood and shudders, after months of carrying
him, this new life with his fierce center, gamboling his year-long summersfull of kicks, until my skin shone,
beat-tight as a drum, until every fragrance had swollen beyond human prick or recognition spurring each
half-grown bone within toward proof that time inside a woman's body burns and multiplies; this same
time gone wild since Connor blazed into our lives*

One of Clara's older daughters was there
last night, at the República Cromañón nightclub.
I picture her sneaking home, her hidden hair

singed, her eyelashes burned off, her ticket stub
tossed off by the laundry, the stub that floated up
through the wash Clara had her arms thrust in, the tub

water gray beside my grandmother's stone washboard's lip
out on the balcony where, like some paper bloom,
the Cromañón ticket, that evidence, floated to whip

Clara's bent back straight into prayer and the rare whim
of expletive, but still she, along with Abuela,
insisted she stay, work. *Qué barbaridad.* That's how I left them—

my son bawling in the playpen, Abuela and Clara
muttering over the clear evidence of treachery,
disobedience, of *gracias a Dios, sobrevivió, la voy a matar*

*cuando regreso a casa . . . shaky gratitude of the mother spared . . . where was the mother of that child in
the elevator, too young for carrying her own? renaming her self Clare de Lune; has her baby flared into the
world? too soon . . . Did her kiss shield our child? For luck, she claimed, wildly plucking at his shirt . . . was
it a kiss of fate he wasn't there, in last night's burn, his skin still silken, intact, unhurt, while all those babies
were caught, hapless as Astyanax on fortune's fire wheel whirling, blowing the dancers like dry leaves
beneath a big top billowing collapse upon its stilts*

I try to shake it off in the innocent heat,
try to refocus on how cool glassed interiors
conceive the purely decorative all along the street.

Concentrate: empty artful parlors, amber hasps, mirrors
surrounding accordions gutted on teak
plinths, antique, cherry stained, their

keys arrayed between swollen ground and ceiling leak
in their rising indoor rain, ivory cool and fine.
In such wet heat, the *carteleros* don't eye boutiques

as they pick through trash. Their carts contain
all their moving rooms, all that wasn't wrecked
after the leak that all that remained

of the national debt would be checked
by a floating peso—then the run on the banks,
exodus for Spain, for France, until the locked

borderlands of the motherlands closed and closed ranks.
A father hands his son finds: a bag of bread;
some boxes of tomatoes, some ripe, some rank;

two bags of bottled glass. They won't beg;
they keep to their class; which only parts
to redistribute what the haves have tugged

out to the curb, while the have-nots implore the carts,
their hands outstretched with something like belief,
while I tell myself a story of how a city translates its hurts

into this set of circulating urban arts, recycler, thief, eyeing the facades with nonchalant ease, each sill,
mullion, and mazy laundry line aloof as if unfazed by their lucky pun on relief for the deathly desperate,
for their feet gaining purchase as fingers reach above, stealing to resell, to put a square meal before the
children growing around cardboard passing for a table . . . the furniture gives way to antiques, and the
apartments above are stocked lovingly and with love, all kinds of bric-a-brac ripe for resale—Abuela's
tango paraphernalia, cigar cases, Lladró statues, Victorian hourglass, first edition Borges, her Atlassa
clock . . . imagine a thief with a thief's luck taking everything but what matters most to her . . . no one falls
from the building's walls, no one is birthed into death through fire, no one is hurt . . .

        I think the story
has some promise, but only because

in January all these streets pass for empty—
Rivadavia, Juan de Perón, Corrientes—
two-thirds of Buenos Aires has fled to the sea,

where umbrellas mushroom dayglow among grass
thronged with sand, each thonged body removed
from its dogs and laundry, left behind with *pasea*

perro and shadow. The buildings shove
past their endings in the rooftops' ongoing limbo—
each population spike of

more tenants riddling brick and rebar low
across the old roof. So the city inches toward the sun,
its various rents in tow.

The city reinvents itself upwards feverishly as sin
and into better air, its fervor as if improvisation
were always the way to turn

desire skyward, *and not the stuff of today's headline, the rough but ready nursery in the crammed unconcern and chaos of that oversold show, as if the dying child of necessity were not there in the lucerne spark, in the stuff of Clara's stiff back, the wrack and mess and yes the barbarity of that burn—fourteen babies in the bathroom, three thousand locked in between twelve and twenty years old; the bass pounded bodies by the hundred beyond that allowed by the fire code. They sold tickets, and they sold more. The excess was barely checked by exits padlocked with filed chain, only two doors open, not enough for laws, not nearly enough for what flared in that hour, the crush of coughing lungs and sour sweat piled up in a panic against locked doors, making of life a toy, the children hemmed in and terrified as those within Troy's walls when the Trojan horse opened to stream out men, full enemies, Queen Andromache clutching to herself the child soon to be thrown from a tower of fire, little prince Astyanax hovering before the door unlocking in the hour, the door swinging open in the singed air*

The queen of Spain called to express

her condolences to the president yesterday,
So many young people. The minister's media address belied
insistence that the locked exits caused the tragedy.

Had all the doors been open, no one would have died.
But the delay was deadly. Too many hours passed for
too many children and their children, delayed

and bored on a bathroom floor,
inventing ways to pass the time,
not imagining some would flare

into unimaginable pain, midwife to death.
Think of the midwife at Connor's
birth, think of Connor's first breath

the way you did when you dragged yourself to the water, your inside so nearly about to turn itself out—
then: pain. Then, the way pain turns you out of time and into blasphemies: your body's; an army tucked,
chins to knees inside an equine ruse's gloom and looming hollow; the men floating far above hearing its
rumbling wheels amid a city's worth of cheers on winds alive. You've always lived in a world of pain, and
can't recall your own name or the man's who did this to you, ripping limb through womb only to stall out.
What you do know—between pains but beyond doubt—is that all that wood gathered and lashed—
drifted, salt honed, beyond dead—and the lifeless horse built out of it screamed when men, full grown and
full of death, hacked and slashed their way out to plunder Ilium—you know because their screams are
hushed whenever your breath slashes into your core, dragging with it the night sky shaken by bass rattling
chains against doors

When I arrive at the national library, *Closed for*

January is posted on the door, its denial a hum
against the building's larger architecture,
its brutalist lean. *Think of the baby that will come,*

the building scolds me, *and the baby here now—you can wait, you have a paper. Don't think of the
infants lost to boredom and its twin, revelry—or is it despair?—locked doors closing ranks around dry
fire like the owner's lies, like thunderheads circumscribing hurricanes' eyes. Don't think of Astyanax,
thrown from Troy's tower. Think of the dimming eyes of Borges, his bravery in the face of coming blindness,
counting his books and birds, even or was it odd?. . . in his "Argumentum Ornithologicum." Think of using
Ariadne's furred thread to prove the existence of God. Think of the brutalist architecture of the building
right here. God—granting, for the purposes of prosecution, your existence—how do you face the infinitely
odd and infinitely uneven nightmares you conjure?*

Solo le pido a Dios . . . but Dios,
¿a quién tu pides? The mute door
stares. *Think of the books, not lost, across*

the lock, eclipsed but accounted for, unlike the flocks
of parrots alighting between pigeons, their bodies reversed,
perfectly aligned, their flaming emerald flicks

the improbable among the common, interspersed.
The city's proximate to the parrots' flyway's limit,
given urban sprawl; or air currents immersed

in warming airstreams; or how air in air
can spin, flip, and tower; or the scale of universe
off course as its creatures scatter

and disperse to swirl around locked doors
allowed on streets escorting life's horizons
near to this new now, this ever

stranger here, knocking, knocking to be let in
or out the door arching between tiny homespun
cage and firefly; Dionysus and his floor; flare and run;

the erratic company of our lurking
sometime shadow and her constant better half,
the sun the sun the sun

Sundial

When night takes
the earth, obelisks lose
their eloquence among all
the other shadows' black wag-
ging tongues. Towers, too, can't
speak time sans their share of sun.
A sundial's life is on daylong loan
from furies in the heart of a star.
So long as some here face into
flame they cast the dun spell
that has our back: you
are you are you are.

Commonplace for all obelisks:

In courting your own shadow,
you wed a pillar of salt;
in following your own lights,
your fall surpasses your fault.

IV.

INTO FLAME

The eggs of fireflies hatch in about three weeks. They spend two years as luminescent larvae and, after several molts, spend a month pupating. The longest-lived adults survive about seven days, so time is of the essence.

—*The Animal Kingdom and the Clock Biological*, Lucille Spovak

Curtains edge the courtyard and flare alive where
ever sparks wander out from years of instar—

They glowed through molts, now flash through air
and all that being grown connotes: this winged lantern, that ar-

dent consort come-hither blinking on an isobar,
some hours breeding, some twilights ajar, then dark—

lasting but fast as glass flash frozen in air, from lava far-
flung along a nuée ardente, that ash en masse on fire berserk-

ing burn down highway, city, harbor, and what stark
charred world can ever emerge in the wake

of a mountain reinventing its mark
on the curving edge of planet. Days break

on curtains beaten; on courtyard stones swept warm;
along a scorched harbor. Soils form.

V.

SOILS FORM

The Mid to Early Late Proterozoic Big Cottonwood Formation, UT, contains some of the oldest known tidal rhythmites. These rhythmites, and the estuarine environment they were deposited in, provide valuable constraints on Earth-Moon orbital mechanics and the paleogeography of the western margin of North America, 900 million years ago.

—research synopsis for "Estuarine Sedimentation and Tectonics in Meso- to Neoproterozoic Utah: New Evidence for Ocean Waters over Southwestern Laurentia," Todd A. Ehlers and Marjorie A. Chan, 1997 Geological Society of America Annual Meeting

Remnant. Purple. Marl. Pine needles sidle underfoot. Upslope a shout rappels down
strata. Here water held commerce with itself, and left this: five kilometer thick hint

of a shore where sea swilled river just before the animal kingdom shivered, annelid and

medusoid, into the world. Still, these stripes, black and white piled in argillite, suggest *zebra*
rather than *tide*. But that world, devoid of Equus, dripped with tides. Here is the fallout:

jet silt trickled from low tide's still water / ashen sand fallen from high tide's rapid currents:

black/white/black: tidal lows and highs: aqueous: in rhythmic stacks. Liquidity tugged lunar
and gone to strata. The geologists pose their pickaxes by the stones' disclosures, lift their

cameras, and snap: two silt and two sand layers represent a single day's two low and two high tides.
The shutter

is triggered, and the aperture has them: individual days and nights *from the Precambrian*,
from when land abutted land in one utter continent, before plants fashioned air,

back when the day was shorter the earth spun faster the moon loomed closer the year wore

longer. Now the planets pour themselves across more orbit and the world is full of eyes.
Once water scattered detritus. Between them, silt and sand settled an edge. Now we measure

leavings, their variable rates. Now our cross-sections illustrate all a fallen grain might tip or

intimate: epoch or eon: neap or ebb. Time is meant by sediment. Time is this streaky visage, is
quartz pounded out in surf all along the living shores, is a thing carried from high,

is this thing suspended, is how it falls. One band of light, one band of dark. Fluvial.

A day rivered like today, but without the canyon traffic. No tusks, no savannahs.
No tilting telescopes. No irate nevadas. Now we apply our fervent machines, where time

is the argon barreling through the vacuum chamber, where time is isotope, is ratio, is

sealed from room, the air the plants put there, in supercooled fluid, which is glass, which
was sand. The spectrometers fit the earth's plates into a clockwork universe. name:

atlas: wait: The zebras reverse the breath of the savannah. weight: The climbers

move up the rock. They powder their fingertips with chalk; name their routes: Black
Monday. Mass Wasting. Times Square. Time is falling everywhere. The climbers slide

into their harnesses, swarm around the rhythmites. They fit their bodies to the rock. The body

stops, modulates its limbs' small distances, arrays its weight from the impressions left by three May
raindrops. Left crimp (fingers curled to tips; tips weighting slate as air weights flame) right
pull (body weight pulling against the palm; all purchase only from this pull) stand

up. Just stand up. Stone invites this choreography, matches every human move.
How can we explain this? What sorcery torques a cliff's relief so that it makes of each
climbing body this symphonic reach? Ionic Bonding. Staggering. The climbers'

rappels collapse centuries, and their falls span what grains outlast: volcano; plasticity;

clastic; a ride hitched across the world on the back of a magma plume; riverbed tincture, riverbed
enigma; estuary. Rivers blast quartz to the sea. The fourth kingdom resumes;

the fifth is pending. The bristlecone reverses the lion's breath. One band of water rushing,

one band of water slack. This is the layer where water began splitting. This is the layer
where atoms unmatched. symphonically: toe-hook: remnant: Making artifacts to touch

the infinite, breathing fireweed all the while. Because I want. A rhythmite in my hand,

palming. Nocturnal. Individual days and nights from back before the world engendered
wings. Raindrops ping across radiant energy. Nanometer. Plates of the earth in tumult.

Animals on the verge. Tectonic. The geologists toss their fossils. The belayers shrug their

slack. Because I want to fit myself to the rock. Because before we walk we must climb.
Because we come into the world weak as the third syllable in look after. Because
of the disheartening for which both up or down hill may be liable. Because of the yawn

of the awful. The climbers slouch up the cliff. The rhythmites herald backflow and crest. The mass
spectrometer raids its samples. The geologists descant. The segment is smudged. My sons

stand up, one, then three years later, the younger. Calenders gambol through seven candled days,

the shifting weeks immortal. I put the rhythmite back, but slightly down slope, in the company of
marl. In the midst of the zebra's gallopade, the mystics fall silent. When will the sixth of life's

kingdoms emerge into the world? What will that life make of us? Ancient days in tiers. Because

the fifth kingdom has chanced us. Time is falling everywhere. The rhythmites suggest an ocean
to the south or west. limpid: testament: remnant: Three circling and encircled spheres.

Because of all the planets, this is the only one that has managed magic in its distance from the sun.

Because I want, very badly, to manage. To fit myself to the right distance, the way
a body harnessed over crevasse will fit itself, precisely, to a moving prayer, itself the

shape of the displaced air. High Life. Alpenback. The ancient shore has slanted to

mountain, myths tucked in its sands, waiting for someone to see them. What are we
waiting for? turn: light bending: carmine: cerulean: because the sun: because life

should outlive us: because the fifth kingdom risks: because the sixth is pending:

Calling Calliope with a Water Clock

Time takes the city's women to bide their births. Birth takes a woman to abide. To bide time by water is to take it. A woman to take it cannot abide: the measured cruelties of taken time. Her labor takes obelisk, clepsydra, breaks off their moving. The infant rides her blood back down to light. The light takes the newborn to a sun. The sun takes the born to a divide:

With the first breath, the child's bloodstream reverses its flow.
From then through the twelfth year, the heartbeat slows through weeks and months.
From the age of thirteen on, most seconds one's own heart beats once.

To take the water is, the Greeks knew, to steal it: *clepsydra* scans as *water thief.* When diviners take on time dividing, do they scan *is* as the *if* in grief?

What, in time's long division, splits story into after and before?
A child's arrival, a parent's fall.
A tower's fall; arrival of war.

The mothers' labors move at the pace of stone. To come into life is to become alone.

And here, though meddling, I can't find the difference. Though observing stealth, can't find divide. When will I stop, in time's flow, stealing the future from the present? Even now I thieve from my sons' lives.

Commonplace for parents: *The days are long and the years fly by.*

VI.

YEARS FLY

In the same breath, shining Hektor reached down / for his son—but the boy recoiled, / cringing against his nurse's full breast, / screaming out at the sight of his own father, terrified by the flashing bronze, / the horsehair crest, / the great ridge of the helmet nodding, bristling terror—so it struck his eyes.

—*The Iliad*, Homer

for Astyanax:
his nurse's song

Lord of the City   Hektor's son   still lives long   before words
   What did you see at Troy's tower today?
Unfathomable   some flyway   locked in the bodies of birds

       sleep just there   then as now   but the prince preferred
         to turn his   eyes wide   away
       fixed fast after   some still wider   orbit of blue before words

so still you were   in my arms today   the air barely stirred
   around your mouth   each breath weigh-
ing in my arms   with a weight   warm as the bodies of birds

       when your father back from battle on Troy's tower recurred
        his armament pure metallic intent   splendor errant and at play
       you cried with terror   purest before words

parents   hard or bright with laughter   the evident inferred
   your father showed his face to embrace you
but he couldn't touch fear   hollow as bones   in the bodies of birds

       so you saw it   some thing slipping in a helmet mirrored
        now slip after the dark   the world can mislay
       sleep is a thing spinning into silence   the guess before words
        you are yet   just a guest   a gust   a rushing hushed
       in the bodies of birds

VII.

THE BODIES OF BIRDS

The January 1, 2011, Argentina earthquake, while of historic 7.0 magnitude, is nonetheless typical of a deep earthquake within one of the many subduction zones around the Pacific Ring of Fire. The earthquake was hardly felt in Santiago del Estero, the provincial capital, where Emilio Abdala, a receptionist at the 14-story Hotel Casino Carlos V, told The Associated Press that nobody felt a thing.

—The Guardian

Borges argued for the existence of God.
  Borges argued for this existence
    before his sight was gone.

This argument called for birds
  and the difficulty of counting very
    many of them with the naked eye,

say, a flock. Their number is definite, but not
  visible, neither even nor odd, or either,
    or both? Hence, God.

How envious I am of all he felt,
  his conviction, the careful touch of
    thread through twilight labyrinths,

the spun warp of faith at every split plinth
  in time, tripping over the eclipsed work
    of the world pushing up the stair,

skies flying off behind mountains in the part
  of rivers that swim back into skies
    or the ocean spilling itself into

the enclosed explosion around which we
  carry out our lives this high
    rise encrusted ring inside

or below stork and starling and lark
  below even this yellow beaked
    automaton emerging from the stark

clock, the cuckoo calling out her new
  hour for house and stair
    well and the world under that,

shining in the dark.

VIII.

IN THE DARK

The toll on the city of January's heat wave and of the annual migration for the beach are evidenced by last night's devastating burglary of the Jean-Jorres neighborhood. The sweep nonetheless left, in the same apartment, an exquisite reproduction of Edgardo Donatto's cigar case and the 1855 bronze clock *Atlassa*, valued recently on the EU's *Antique Roadshow* at $25,000.00.

Atlassa is a rare example of swing clocks, which hide their clockworks and emphasize their pendulums. The winged figure of a woman in a revealing draped dress holds the large clock ball in her right hand. How the clock works is not really a mystery. The clock mechanism is inside the ball. When wound, the pendulum moves back and forth for about eight days, at which point the clock needs rewinding.

—*La Nación*

On the mantel half-
way down the hall
an angel holds a toll-
ing world aloft as if

it were entirely safe
no trouble at all
to lift the full
gross and scope of

it even in past-
prime real estate
in the plumbed
heart of Buenos Aires

even with the added weight
of this ticking moon (its
orbit jammed the way (some-
times) desire's is)

IX.

TIME'S DESIRE

Las Vegas, first settled for its springs, is the fastest growing city in the United States, in what is now the driest desert in the United States. Lake Mead, the ultimate source of water for the Las Vegas Valley, could run dry by 2021.

—Scripps Institute

I have fears re: loneliness   and yet in this Mojave   when I
consider the colossal century   this seems absurd
sands stretch toward boundless Vegas   old gods rule   read: multiply

      lonely is oasis   lonely is mirage   lonely is an eye
      sore   lonely is after   mostly during   a bit before any word
      or letter   i.e. "I"   when I have fears about loneliness I

wonder whether even exile would be worse   I
mean   at least exile requires first   a chummy herd
O Wild Fire Regime   O Ancient O Measure O Multipli

      er   O Exile rebelling from exile   how would you prophesy
      against comfort and commandment   unheard and unprepared
      as the lonely re company   and yet fruits fear not the lonely eye

mourn not their seeds in the face of grim futurity   the great lie
of sibilant sibling certainty   My darlings we were undeterred
in having you two   though I knew and knew better than to multiply

      along the lines of some outdated testimony that would give the lie
      to a god outgrown by our own excesses so extravagantly shared

      Can that god be lonely, now   What world can await us many   Yet when I

      think of that blur burden crowd   it teems its charactery *Multiply*

X.

MULTIPLY

Intermediate in behaviour between a lava flow and an ash fall is the glowing avalanche of a nuée ardente. A nuée ardente caused the total destruction of the city of St. Pierre on the island of Martinique in 1902, killing about 30,000 inhabitants.

—*Petrology*, Ernest G. Ehlers and Harvey Blatt

Fathoms beneath us, sea and fire make fine lace of stone.
Midnight surfaces: cold, wet, cast in a furnace of stone.

Rumor turned St. Pierre out—*the hermits are on parade*—
a lone crab lingers by the sea, courts a carapace of stone.

Come lent, snakes and insects take to same streets
where rivers of rum on fire once ran to the embrace of stone.

Listening Hélène opened the cages of her cricket and fireflies,
then mourned their loss alone, her jewels mute in their case of stone.

Clare's letters write of snakebites, fatal to a child:
Fifty children laid in earth this week, each perfect face of stone.

The ascension started slow that May: fumarole and fog.
The penitent thronged confession late in panic's place of stone.

After, the cathedral prophesied those in Riga, Coventry, Rome.
Rain in the organ pipes. Ironwork. Altar of air, rosace of stone.

They say columbine needs earth to grow, or the human heart.
The monk whispers inside this wall, amen. Or grace of stone—

Cyparis was drunk again when they tossed him in the cell.
Fire from a mountain killed 30,000 while he slept in a space of stone.

Other towers climb steep air clockwise, biding their understood enemy
—one thousand right hands moored by a staircase of stone—

not so, Pelée's obelisk. Inside the lava dome: a year of fire
flared cerise nightly higher aspiring apex, failed brace of stone.

An island arc might develop: listen to the serpentine
hiss, giving up its light and rains in the green race of stone.

What can one give the unborn? What does a namesake want?
Give her mountains, Alina. And other things unmade at the pace of stone.

String

Cerro Torre   penultimate pitch   in spasms   five climbers clipped in   don't think of deep cold
colonizing yesterday's face   focus on   five star points of pain   all moving in place

Ice axe   serac   smear   half lip   tunnel   tower   sugar snow   organ pipe   immobilized tornado
at this dangling angle   the pentatonic scale falls across us   arranges us   let's say as Aeolian harp

chasing yesterday we hang here waiting for Hektor   waiting for Achilles for Priam for that fawn
Patroklus for even labyrinthine Odysseus and his winnowing fleet his   faithful flea-ridden Argos

because they fell in spectacle's savage tantrums   we can expect them   any minute now
dipped in their bronze rhyme   their immortality our foolish mouth sounds   from
their original deep time   if I fall they'll be along

if I litter the height *la escoba de Dios* might sweep us   into one day's worth   of web page song

everything is rimed   sight is half-blind   to stare is to tear   to hang is to curl   to put to thin
air an   opening question   mark   to a question   out there   appealing the dark

Que espera Andromache   Que espera Briseis   Que espera Hecuba Scamandrius   Que espera his
unnamed nurse *Que espera Cassandra* and her ravings   entire sun-tipped migrations chasing her
words from receding futurity   *Que espera Chrysaor   Que espera* the armies of domestics
laborers more migrant workers more   and more the moving center of whenever castle   stalled at
the edges of song

A minute a minute *la escoba de Dios*

Que esperan los pájaros   Que esperan los caballos   Que esperan todos los ciervos que no
comienzan guerras   Que esperan   las plantas   las piedras   la oscuridad

Que compensa sus sacrificios

Can we decide whom to wait for   wait that's not what I meant
el viento   el viento   y el viento   tocando nuestras cardeñas   what I meant
Que estamos esperando   the wind is sweeping the lace   from which we hang
threads of sky inconstant   sifting shifts into zero   just off a continent   dispersed

Commonplace for physicists: *The winds of change gust through an aeolian universe.*

XI.

ARIADNE, AEOLIAN

M-Theory in 11 dimensions is the mother of all strings. And that theory works perfectly fine . . . in dimensions beyond 11, we have problems with stability, these theories are unstable, they decay back down to 11 dimensions, they have what are called anomalies, singularities, which kill an ordinary theory. So the mathematics itself forces you to 11 dimensions.

—Michio Kaku

mother's long logic   now kinked   two turns past praise
            or blame   not quite committed   still a thing felix
the culpa   unanswerable   though this is what stays

            his thunder   his beckon   the turn of his phrase
is a corridor   a consequence   a creature   a mix
            half brother   half hearted   half blame   half praise

half hearted prayers turn so many ways
            in every man   his own god   some backdoor heroics
a dark hall   a pale thread   and this is what stays

            a small thing pointing trumps the maze
three left turns quicken   one right turn tricks
            both assume understanding   blame   praise

I gave him his way back   this river rushes both ways
            to sea   to source   the waves mix   their rhythmics
self-silence   he has left me with water   and this is what stays

            at the end of my story   a god   comes to this shore always
he takes me   always he's warm   always he tricks
            the river's turnoffs   to crown rounding   praise
what night   what tightening   what spins out   what stays

Electron

    proposition: *energy is eternal delight*
    proposition: *energy is matter times*
    light's speed   times   the speed of light

can this frame   be relative   when what
weeps are two children whose comfort rhymes
with their company: *energy is eternal delight*

    a wood block   Orpheus translates
    into Blake   burning angels' names
    into bodies of trees   *bodies of light*

true as SETI   calling every night
everyone   no one   whom-
ever's out there   *energy is eternal delight*

    how to explain   this radical isolate
    in which we float if not   that a time bomb
    gets set   in every vicinity   of $e = mc^2$

counting down each planet's days   to shared night
weep Eurydice   for his eye   alight   now a first atom
smashing into turn   into elegy's eternal shore of eternal delight
forever on the other side   your matter spins out its crash into   light
        times light

XII.

WHAT SPINS OUT

The second is the duration of 9,192,631,770 periods of the radiation corresponding to the transition between the two hyperfine levels of the ground state of the caesium-133 atom.

—resolution taken by the thirteenth General Assembly of the
Conférence Générale des Poids et Mesures in October 1967

for Caesium

Disperse, wavelet.

      Of all the alkalis with their roguish loner husks,

their single shells, you are the only atom

              with this hyperfine spin flip,

       your taste for photons is the most cooperative, your solo

electron whorls at the aptest distance

             from the forceful core

      for easy escape. Your farthest charge acts as if a trapeze

           perpetually swung toward it out of the gloomy corner,

as if it were elegantly costumed in your name, nothing garish but suitable for flying: bluish,

  gray.

            And there is your outermost now,

               spunky at the brink of its probability cloud,

           waving lavishly, as if warming to the pace of our impending

volley, or preparing its patience for this lesson, the explanation of your special devouring,

                  palming the chalk to describe

                      how you can be at once

          all this slippery mosso orbit and somnolent in arms.

for Caesium:
Astyanax's swinging cousin Cassandra's song

Creatures stream creatures to arrive at this:

      awe, some art, a backward glance,

civilization measured by its best hexametric

      discontents then finally just the measure,

its lingering hunger for any constant thing, for certain

      company in an unstable clearing,

where one rubs its rarity a bit timidly,

      counting constancy's instances on one

hand: Light's alacrity. Universal pull.

      Some charge we neither see nor feel.

While time, in turn, turns in-

      constant. Its unruly arrival

goes on in one while origins skip

      nimbly into dark, trailing three hundred million

meters of light—this, an instant's distance.

      Another: per second, the planet

reflected in human eyes

      plunges thirty thousand meters into dark

as ten darks fall and ten darks rise

across each blinking iris. Breathable seconds

fill one's lungs with thirteen hundred

milliliters of air. Audible seconds,

though, one hears in silence—

between sound and echo—

that gap ten times. The alkalis, hospitable,

welcome the second

into its element:

9,192,631,770 caesium cycles. And as for flight,

a hummingbird's wing beats

seventy times while, by chance

or coincidence, we partake of a nonce

improbable: as the moon

slips away from (to return to)

the months, most seconds

one's own heart beats once.

for Astyanax's hummingbirds:
what Andromache saw him see

when you hover at your nectar you detain the human heart

—our poor blood-flooded muscle ponderous as mud

chambers dragging magma while your wings let fly, splicing end from end, start from start—

pinion tips to dip easily seventy times

seventy times to peak across the bars' confine

before our staggered heart can beckon its reluctant blood

to measure remember reckon hearken mark

even one piece of passing time

detain then the starlings

contain the avocets

untangle scores of shorebirds from the fishers' nets

Priam's walls still stack their ashlar's lean against sky

before my baby's birthday

I will invent an aviary

its rungs so finely wrought they can stall starlight

let Hektor select his yearlings

        let him suppose his son will live long enough

                to carry on

marauding through the night

        let him expect his mother's prayers

                shield him

from torchlight

        let him banish Hecuba and her train to pray

                each day

he springs from his chariot

        home—let him imagine prayers can be measured

                in warm blood

on warm breath

        let him wish lists of supplicants

                in fine thread

loomed vast

        let him imagine a prayer to outlast one

                thousand masts

and sails unfurled

        let him guess some mothers' prayers out-

                weigh

the world

        your son has seen a stone outweigh your reason

                beloved

and all words are

        already outnumbered   your son has seen

                how much

greater

        it may be to gather these unsung but humming   birds

for Astyanax:
what his nurse saw him see

We walk through the aviary, alive. Through layers
              of cage and avocet, your gaze finds the swing set. We circle
the birds, take up second place in the line. The shadow of an older, more vocal cousin
     falls and rises across us. You are not so sure,
                  though you are seduced by the swing, caught somewhere between

     a soul flashing past its battlements

                   —recurrence, timbre, and return—and
     a creature clinging terror to his white-

armed mother lately when
              ever his father recurs
                   upon Troy's watchtower

bronze-and-horse-hair-armored.   His helmet cons,
                his helmet vexes
                shoring up another son, that one monstrous
                     as some pyrite sun
              streaking mean heat lightning utterly snuffed
                  by melting the Aegean's beach to bronze.

Yesterday you glimpsed him

swimming in the helmet's surface

your twin from where he's hidden

where misshapen, poor as any thing that breaches between you and the beloved face—

as *any* impoverished ongoing instant—*between*—you and

your father as he flees Achilles

ringing Troy's walls,

three times past Scamander's double

springs, the one throwing steam, the other cracking ice, three times the champions glance

past the wind-lashed fig—

your father's flight
drags out this
deliberate
even serene dis-

tance between two
bodies—little,
this interval,
but still so

pitilessly
tranquil that swift
Achilles can
only capture

the gap's exact
madding measure
in the rawhide
tether he cuts

to tie Hektor
one second be-
hind grief's riot-
ing chariot

I saw you see past your father

                  ice-silent

                                sand-dragged

                       the Aegean's crystals

                         billowing as you dove

                            after, the ashlar

                streaking walls or clouds

                                mean with heat lightning—

       the helmet's twin reached for you

                       I held you as you screamed

when he reaches past you

on top of the tower

the winds' singed whipping will

caution your fall but still little prince

I saw you hold each second

slowed to this sight:

when your brilliantly armored father falls outside his father's quartz-rimed walls

it will have been fired

within his prince's ring

that twin's bronze touch

your candent tandem falling

I held your pain-shattered mother

while Hektor drove his horses through their paces

through his father's city's

feasting halls

where the vineyards teem

where figs crowd figs

his stallions' hooves trampled the vats, their shanks grape splattered

even the yearlings

flashed past the walls

tendering their paces through Scamander's

double springs

water-bodied furies

plashing tourmaline.

Your father rode bare headed that morning

I saw you both born,

and still I saw it too, your invisible twin. It is yours, and only fate:

born with us all the second we are born.

for Caesium:
Cassandra's song

They say the second you were born you bore the second.
They say a drawbridge is moat before span.
They say you are at least that stable.
They say a drawbridge is amassed before moat.
They say, in small spaces, you live large.
They say—they swear—you split the second.
They say this splitting is bound up in a charge:
bridge drawn; bridge down.
They say you invented it in books you never wrote.
They say you are the largest atom still stable.
They say a drawbridge is a spell reversed.
They say you have fifty-five electrons.
They say you split the second from the first.
They say the first was blue and very old.
They say a drawbridge is a plank unwalked.
They say they'll drag the plank to the pyre across sand.
They say a moat can crack like leaves in the cold.
They say the second now is old and nearing blue.
They say less in the end than they talk.
Their talk is wilder than the end is old.
I've heard the rumors: you melt at pristine temperatures.
I understand what I can expect from you:
even if you could be held in my hand,
you would drip through my fingers like liquid gold.

for Astyanax:
what Helen saw him see

a horse made of driftwood and ships

all along each piece
        movement sparks
                driftwood records

swirl and eddy
        the ribcage is seven ripples
                their fits and starts

the right hip arises
        from murmur remembered
                the mane emerges

a revel of trickles
        slick in oak
                the backbone

drumlin or flood
        and all this moss sand
                and once-wood

is sunset bronzed
        so along the way
                each curve lies

the light both swarms
        and stellifies
                a horse

made of bronzed waves
        weighing one
                ton of light only

the face
        recedes still
                further into

stillness
        but the body
                emerges and keeps

emerging the body
        keeps moving
                in place

for Astyanax:
what Hecuba saw him see

Horses by the hundred await your father's break-
ing, and still the war, marooned, plunges dully on,
past bronze, past iron, moored in rust. Twelve
daughters' dowries given or received (we've
kept our girls close, so what counts as cost?); old
Priam is nine years closer to his end—

aren't we all?—but I see death dogging him, lend-
ing the lie to stone each time daybreak
slants across his walls. Priam named his death "Hektor"
on the day your father was born—*this son*
among fifty, defender of the city. But Priam also won't believe
this tangle of fates could involve

Hektor's death: botched hospitality; the impossible resolve
of goddesses scorned; an awkward friend-
ship with love's lure or reward—that girl we receive
and receive and receive as if beauty didn't habitually break
or raze or besiege whoever takes it in—poor Helen
must bear hers but the rest of us behold—

and it is worse to witness. Andromache told
me she spied your father choosing for you twelve
more foals. How he has always insisted on
calling you Scamandrius, while the rest defend
your name as Astyanax—*Lord of the City*—which breaks
your father's heart, your mother told me. I believe

her; she believes your father; your father grieves
at what all this belief must mean: that one barely one day old
has his life subsumed to a sign. Birth can't break
or end a war, but war's red barbarity absolves
the breaking of a baby in whose blood Troy's splen-
dor runs abundant, coursing nascent occasion

for a whole city's hope (or an old woman's mon-
ologue). As long as you are alive we can believe
your father lives, and lives by the thousand depend
on his—a single slender thread of fire holding
back lions, their patience by ten or twelve
winters eaten—the way any windbreak

grows olive groves—the way my mother's features break
across your face, the present putting on
the past—the spring she died (twelve
springs ago) the birds fell silent, but did not leave.
Now they follow their song, and all Troy's gold—
however finely wrung by Andromache's wish—won't end

their abandoning. Though she's detained pieces of their sound,
and all we hear would urge belief that daybreak
has broken between the sky's frozen gold
and a town's penned gilded trilling. But dawn
halved and landed turns on itself or moribund. We've
offered to the gods—our best wine, twelve

tender ocher heifers in each shrine, twelve
times twelve yearlings never broken or branded—
now the animals scatter when incense begins; I've

prayed until I can't remember for what—*break*
this or that headlong terror's killing streak—amnesia more sudden,
less explicit of late—amnesia nags while memory scolds

that tomorrow you will turn one year old,
and Cassandra—almost twelve,
though she still sees you as a cousin—has given
Priam her promise to give you her swing. End-
ing her swinging will, he hopes, break
her of her babble—but the sight won't leave

her so easily—it cleaves
to the body it's chosen, ice clear and as cold.
Cassandra caught me today at daybreak
just as I started to let your starlings go—of our twelve
daughters, she's always been the one to mend
my plans—adorable, dire scion—the one to look on

as the starlings hovered, returned to alight on
their perches. We opened all the pens. They won't leave,
now, until the end.
Their quiet will keep yours company. They told
me what you would see at the tower, twelve
springs after my mother's body was taken by the breakwater:

War itself will break around the body Hektor abandons.
His chest will open. Out will fly twelve siegeless days, a peace in
pieces, each holding its ends: on the eve of battle, the rhapsodes begin.

for Astyanax swinging
beside his swinging cousin

the swing arcs against the sky: our shadows touch: now trifoliate: how lucky we

are: now separate: the avocets' contained rush: their calm a garbled green: reticence or nest:

these were their beaches, these their sands, this change not theirs:

cousin: memory works its best necromancies on what has passed,

elegant hope knows only *now*—hosted at mobile hearths—

so our city will end before your memory begins but you've always been most within the city

that will always be

the innermost remembrance of all subsequent cities:

since ours, every polis will know itself to be no more and no less than

some welcome undone: a scale cast massive

descending toward waste: tumult: caprice:

when the winds thicken sufficiently with Troy's sands

      you will watch twelve winds made visible

            as shifting paths of sand

cousin: when you leave us: trust the winds: when they rise

      a mistral-rippled atlas will crystallize

            between Scaean tower and horizon,

      an aeolian embodied roughly but enough

        to collect those amply small to slip through

the Aegeans' inexorable ruse: spectacle's savage tantrums:

            Troy's last son thrown as if by muses from the tower

      —no continent of solace, no Rome can recover this—

but cousin: what if: you can be

      caught by recollection—your first—of this second

                   —*now*—

breaks the fall

—*now*—

                    weaves it back

      to rising: strings: sky trussed: memory's tether: a swing:

sand remembers its several selves once they blur: blown to flowing glass
breakers muster a shore's nomad rigors to blast a mountain's substance from its adamance

orogeny's origin's ruin floats in foams' salt lace and silicates: each grain itself sun fast
storms recall oceans' gloaming when they cast rain looming through fathoms of air

maps cannot fathom a world misremembered as small flat scattered and far

see there, beyond

     the edge of the swing   the god

                    that can exist
                    only in its creation

     so a city holds itself in all cities: a glass holds itself in sand:

                  ride the hollow

                    of your land's wind-pulled

                  remembrance

        summon this second:

                  between
                    climbing and diving

cousin you are far enough into life

                by a second

                                  that you will always float

                                                  through the world

      not quite weighting

          your skeleton,

          your diving reflex half-asleep,

                a festival of oxygen, all your rosy

             riotous flow somehow also

         the bob of a swing

     pulsing out of   all the time in this tilted world

the swing's found now   arc aloft   Aeolian

string humming another string's rhyme:

a song   a piece   silence   a prince   a child unfurled in time

Acknowledgments

Many thanks to University of Arizona Press, for their faith and support in bringing out my first poetry collection, *torch song tango choir.*

Thanks to the journals in which sections of the current book-length poem first appeared, sometimes in slightly altered forms and under different titles:

Alpinist: "Soils Form" as "The Mid to Early Late Big Cottonwood Formation"

Carolina Quarterly: "Night Takes the Earth" as "Laminar Flow"

Colorado Review: "Years Fly" as "Nurse Song for Astyanax"

cream city review: "Ariadne, Aeolian" as "Ariadne, Off the Island"

Denver Quarterly: "For Caesium" as "Letter to Caesium" from "What Spins Out" ("Disperse, wavelet" and "They say the second you were born you bore the second")

Dogwood: "Calling Calliope with a Midwife's Doppler" as "Dialing Calliope with a Doppler"; "The Bodies of Birds" as "Subduction 1/1/11"

EPOCH: "Obelisk" from "The Keeping of Time"

Kenyon Review: "Time's Desire" as "Lake Mead Ticker Tape"

Measure: "Horse Made of Driftwood and Ships" as "The Driftwood Horse" from "What Spins Out"

Prairie Schooner: "For Astyanax: what Hecuba saw him see" as "Hecuba's Song for Astyanax" from "What Spins Out"

Sand Canyon Review: "Glass Remembers Sand" as "Hourglass/11:11"; "For Astyanax's hummingbirds" from "What Spins Out"

The Iowa Review: "In the Dark" as "Sonnet" and "Into Flame" as "Firefly"

Thanks

Many thanks to those who nurtured this book through its infancy: Karen Brennan, Peter Covino, Katherine Coles, and Kathryn Bond Stockton. Immeasurable thanks to Jacqueline Osherow, who in equal measure bears witness and praise; to Tom Stillinger, whose "some epics" class wed me to a better future; and to Barry Weller, guide past and guide lasting through (for starters) Homer.

Much gratitude to those who helped bring out this version of the book, especially to Kristen Buckles, Holly Schaffer, Leigh McDonald, and Diana Rico.

Love and gratitude to Corinna Vallianatos and Kevin Moffett for their compass and company; to Jessica Lewis Luck for keeping together poetry and adventure; and especially to Nicole Walker, whose words and work keep writing in my weeks and poetry in the night. Special thanks to Juan Delgado for a decade of showing me the way. Thanks to my students for their teachings and to my colleagues for their convictions.

Colossal thanks to my parents, Jan and Julia Nogues Paegle, for giving me time.

Unending love to my sons, Connor and Quinn, for keeping time open.

Love and admiration to my niece Alina for her artistry and my nephew Kurt for his acrobatics.

A world of gratitude to my sisters, Rita and Christina Paegle, for everything, every day.

And always, for Steve: *quel giorno più non vi leggemmo.*

About the Author

Julie Sophia Paegle's first book of poems, *torch song tango choir,* was selected as one of the premiere debuts of 2010 by Poets & Writers and won recognition in the International Latino Book Awards, a Utah Arts Council Award, and others. She teaches at California State University, San Bernardino, where she directs the MFA program. She lives in the San Bernardino Mountains with her husband, Stephen Lehigh, their sons, Connor and Quinn, and their menagerie.